THEY LOVE US

Written and illustrated by Robert L. Leslie

Copyright © 2016 Robert Laurie Leslie
All rights reserved.

ISBN-13: 978-1533662736

ISBN-10: 1533662738

Book Layout and Formatting by James Ian Montbriand
Author of Illustrated Short Stories about Tall Masted Ships from the Sailing Era.

DEDICATION

I would like to dedicate this book to my family. First and foremost to my wife Carmen who has supported me in all my adventures. I would also like to give a huge heartfelt hug to all my children Aimee, Elyse and Andrew who gave me the inspiration to create this book.

FOREWORD

As a father the world can seem like a frightening place. My only prayerful wish was that our children would find trust and peace in the world that surrounded them. They say it takes a village to raise a child. I realize now that it's not the size of the village that matters, but the unselfish heart that shares its love. The inspiration that comes from children is the need to be needed. The true challenge in life is not to overcome our fears, but to find the True Love that will help us face them.

PLANTING THE SEED OF UNSELFISH LOVE

MY FAMILY LOVES EACH OTHER...

... that is what families do.

MY PARENTS LOVE US...

...they need to love.

DAD LOVES ME...

... he taught me to fish.

I KNOW HE LOVES ME...

... when I fall down, he cries.

DAD AND I SPEND TIME TOGETHER...

... I love my dad.

MOTHER LOVES ME...

...we dance together.

WHEN I FEEL SICK...

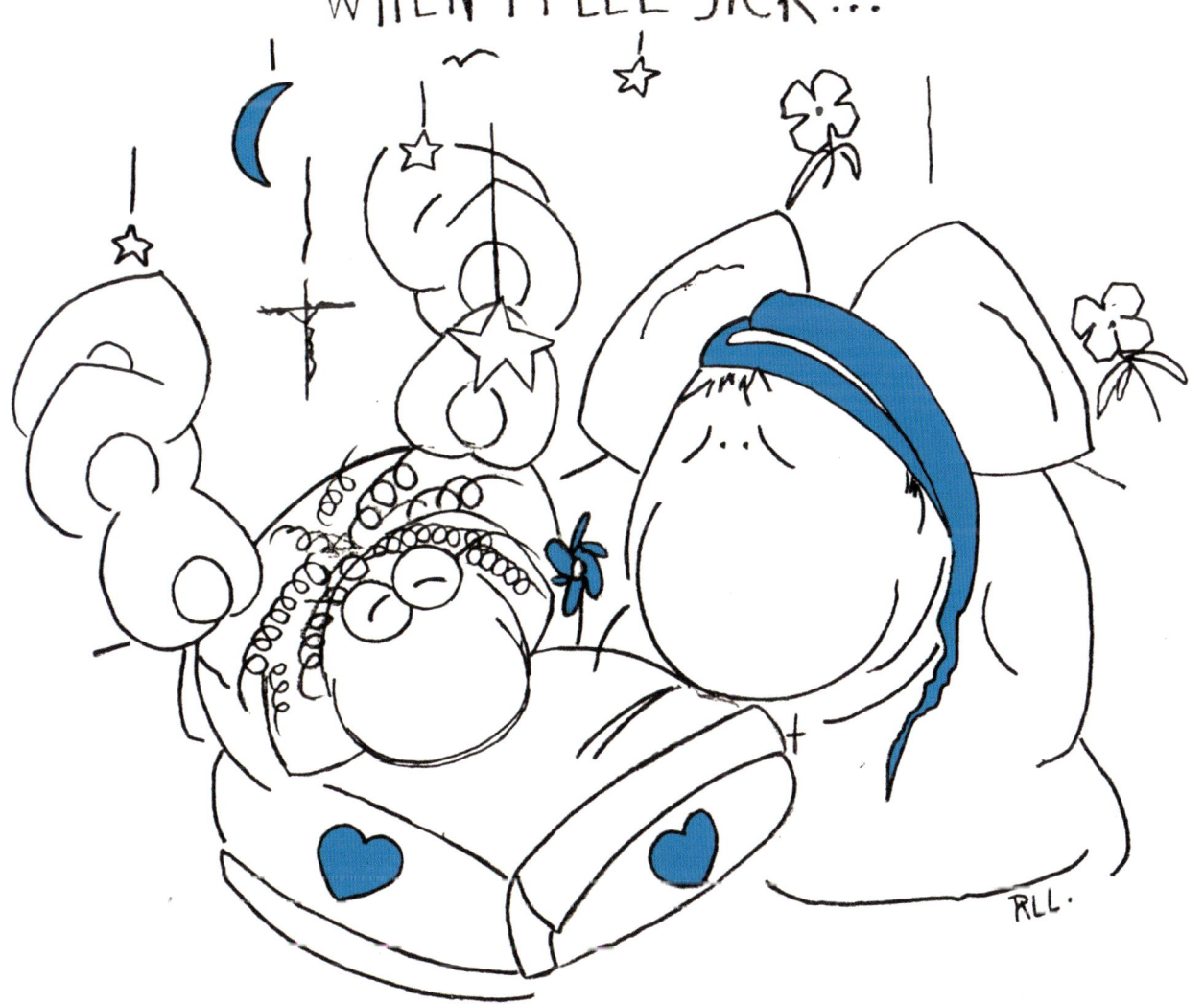

...she watches over me.

I AM MY MOTHER'S LITTLE FLOWER...

... she is the gardener.
I love my mother.

WE LOVE OUR DOG ...

... she is never too busy to listen.

OUR DOG LOVES US...
...we are never too busy to play.

MY GRANDPARENTS LOVE US...

...they love each other.

GRAMPA LOVES ME...

...he tells me stories about days gone wiser. I love grampa.

MY GRANDFATHER LOVES US...
... he promised us a love that would never die.

GRAMMA LOVES ME...

...I hold her hand when she is feeling lonely.

WHEN I AM LONELY...

...she holds my hand.

I LOVE MYSELF...

... I feel loved.

MY BROTHER LOVES ME...

...when he plays with his friends, he says, "It is alright if she comes."

THE BABY LOVES ME...

... I make her laugh.

WHEN YOU SHARE YOUR DREAMS...

...you share your love.

WHEN YOU SHARE YOUR LOVE...

... anything is possible.

Let's create a world without fear. RLL

"We can easily forgive a child who is afraid of the dark. The real tragedy of life is when an adult is afraid of the light."

— Plato

ABOUT THE AUTHOR

Robert Laurie Leslie was born on April 30, 1957. He was raised in Regina, Saskatchewan, Canada. Second son of a Scottish immigrant (William Laurie Leslie) and French Canadian mother (Armande Leone Labreche). Robert graduated from Martin Collegiate in 1975. After finishing a three year Student Guidance Association Program from the University of Saskatchewan, he went on to achieve his Barbering and Cosmetology Certificates from SIAST Institute in Saskatoon, Saskatchewan. Married in 1983, Carmen and Robert opened Ohara Hair Studio and with the growing love of three children, the journey began. For the next thirty years Robert's passion for Life and Love developed through artistic expression. Now at 59, Robert has come to accept that the journey he now shares with his family is one they never have to face alone. And with every word that he writes, he thanks Jesus, Son of God, He's a part of it.

Made in the USA
Charleston, SC
17 October 2016